I0371409

The Broken Cauldron

Lorna Smithers

The Broken Cauldron

Lorna Smithers

This work CC-BY-NC-SA 2021 Lorna Smithers
All reproductions must be for non-commercial use only, must bear attribution to the author, and must carry this same license.

ISBN: 978-1-7357944-4-0

Gods&Radicals Press
an imprint of RITONA a.s.b.l
3 Rue de Wormeldange
Rodenbourg, Luxembourg
L-1695

Layout and Design: Rhyd Wildermuth
Cover Image: Tom Brown (hopelessmaine.com)

View our catalogue and online journal at
ABEAUTIFULRESISTANCE.ORG

For
the Head of Annwn,
Old Mother Universe
and all who have died
by the broken cauldron
and the flashing sword.

'Imagine if you can't remember.'
Charlotte Hussey

'History doesn't really 'repeat itself,'
but it's full of repeating forms.'
Rhyd Wildermuth

'He records the constellation in which his own epoch
comes into contact with that of an earlier one.'
Walter Benjamin

Contents

The Star Cauldron

'Is it not the cauldron of the Head of Annwn...
A ridge about its edge and pearls.
It will not boil the food of a coward,
that has not been sworn...'
The Spoils of Annwn

Returning not on time
but at the perfect time
to the place I made my vow,
your cauldron of pouring water
is still flowing and today
it contains the stars.

As always I have a question,
tearing through the veil
torn a million times,
calling through the names
and faces of indefinite thoughts,
impelled by a shape and form unsung:

the suggestion of a Bardic book
prompted by a voyage
to the moon in the river
where I stood amongst your stars

and in the rain of their fire learnt
the Awen only follows absolute necessity.

You say, "Do what is necessary.
Write the book that needs to be written.
The stars in my cauldron; write it in their fire."

Introduction

Two years ago my patron deity, Gwyn ap Nudd, a ruler of Annwn[1], showed me a cauldron filled with stars. The next time I saw it, it was broken. This inspired a quest to understand the significance of the broken cauldron in ancient British mythology.

The myths I studied[2] were penned in medieval Wales but are rooted in an older oral tradition. All tell the story of the cauldron: the womb of Ceridwen, a goddess I have come to know as Old Mother Universe. Traditionally the cauldron symbolises inspiration, wisdom and rebirth. When it is broken or stolen, cataclysmic consequences are unleashed.

As I journeyed deeper into these myths and was called to consider how they relate to ecological disasters, the fragmentation of meaning, the oppression of women, chemical and biological warfare and atomic energy, I became increasingly certain of their relevance for today.

My attention was drawn to the violence of Arthur's raid on Annwn and assault on its inhabitants. The moment Lleog thrusts his flashing sword into the cauldron came to symbolise the patriarchal worldview which has dominated Western Europe for nearly two thousand years and is founded on the oppression of the Other.

1. *The Ancient British Underworld*

2. *See Bibliography*

Therefore, I have endeavoured to tell the stories of others: marginalised figures overshadowed, oppressed, or slaughtered by Arthur and his court. Some of the pieces are written from my perspective and some speak from other viewpoints.

By re-telling the story of the broken cauldron I aim to show how it relates to our current crises as a warning from the gods and storytellers and as a wake-up call.

I.
The Broken Cauldron and the Flashing Sword

The Broken Cauldron

In June 2015 I participated in a writing workshop with Sarah Hymas based around the 'Understanding the Ritual' exhibition at The Storey in Lancaster, which was inspired by shamanistic traditions. Sarah prompted us to use techniques such as writing in the voice of an artwork and journeying into that work to find its origins.

I chose a painting by Sumit Sarker called 'Nymphs1e7.' This stood out due to the sheer contrast between the blackness of the ocean from which the nymphs emerged and their shining eyes, molten and tear-bright. It also gripped me as a vision of a possible future.

The story it told was of an oil spill in rising seas which had consumed everything but a fog-surrounded, lightning-plagued bastion. Despairingly, I found myself posing a random stream of questions; "All the houses are gone?" "All the washing lines?" "All the gardens?" - "*Everything.*"

Yet, more hopefully, when I communed with the nymphs they told me of their birth from a tear in the North Sea. They came, "Speaking not silent to release the fire of the impossible." They also said, "There has always been a beginning."

Still shaken by this vision of environmental catastrophe, the next morning I consulted Gwyn. He told me its source was "The Broken Cauldron."

I was suddenly transported to a land where a cauldron lay in huge and broken shards. From it poured poisoned streams.

Horses drinking at their banks collapsed, foaming at the mouth, convulsing, sweating themselves into the hills. Amongst them walked a long-legged man trying to numb their pain with whispers in their twitching ears. When their eyes dulled and glazed he wept.

I recognised this scene from *The Story of Taliesin*. I was looking upon the cauldron of Ceridwen, shattered as a result of Gwion Bach's carelessness tending her magical brew. Whilst Gwion escaped with three drops of pure Awen[3] the rest of the mixture became poison and killed the horses of Gwyddno Garanhir.

I stood on the last remnant of Gwyddno's land to escape the inundation after Seithenin and Mererid failed to close the flood gates. The land where Gwyn appeared to Gwyddno on the brink of death and escorted him to Annwn. The land where, in my lifetime, a storm has exposed the petrified forest that gave rise to the story of Cantre'r Gwaelod and burst bankings have revealed the weir where Taliesin was found. A land threatened by rising sea levels.

For the first time I had made a genuine connection with *The Story of Taliesin*.

My inability to connect with it once troubled me, because it is seen by most Druid orders as central to the Bardic Tradition: Gwion's transformations as he flees from Ceridwen, and his rebirth from her womb, represent initiation. Instead of identifying with Taliesin I felt like Avagddu 'Utter Darkness,' Ceridwen's son for whom the potion was brewed but got none: a dark outsider looking in.

3. *Divine inspiration*

And I am still an outsider watching with horror as Gwion escapes with the Awen and Gwyddno's horses perish in the poison. Recognising the terrible price of three drops of inspiration...

Whilst Taliesin is venerated by Druids as the spirit of the Awen incarnate, slipping effortlessly between worlds and forms, little attention is paid to the cost his theft exacts on the land and its inhabitants.

This is paralleled in his later life. Taliesin shamelessly and sycophantically sings the praises of northern warlords in return for riches and mead as the Brythonic kingdoms fall. His reckless determination to steal, with King Arthur, the cauldron from the Head of Annwn results in the deaths of hundreds of men.

Taliesin epitomises all that is questionable and dislikeable about the Bardic Tradition. I would rather identify with Avagddu than with the thief who refuses to learn from his mistakes and whose selfish greed can only lead to the world's end as Ceridwen swallows everything.

I would rather walk my own path in devotion to Gwyn and the spirits of the land than be complicit in the mysteries of Taliesin.

Like Avagddu, Gwyn is a god who haunts the peripheries of the Bardic Tradition. He appears in liminal times and places to guide the dead and holds back their fury lest it destroy thisworld.

His world is Annwn: 'not-world,' 'the deep.' There he keeps a cauldron that is whole and filled with stars: the infinite reflection of the womb of Old Mother Universe, Ceridwen.

Gwyn offers the possibility of fixing the broken cauldron by gathering the poison back into it from the land. Retrieving the spilled stars, the 'fire of the impossible', the unknown stories of those who perished ignominiously. Telling them back to the universe to sate the fury of the spirits of Annwn and soothe Ceridwen's wrath.

Gwyn's Star Cauldron is not a prize to be won, but represents a task to be performed. A way of amending Taliesin's mistakes. This will not be fulfilled in my lifetime and may never be fulfilled. But, like the star-bright nymphs emerging from a tear in the oil-slick seas before the northern fortress, it offers a glimpse of a new beginning.

The Head of Annwn Addresses Arthur's Raiding Party

This pearl-rimmed cauldron within the earth filled with stars and jewels; how alluring it is, how you long for it. What will you learn from its mysteries? Has it not already given you enough dark secrets? Secrets that could destroy your world?

What lies in the cauldron now you have done away with the knowledge of wise women? Split the witches in half? Killed the giants? Driven to the seas the most ancient of boars? You are on the wrong quest, looking for the wrong grail, the cure-all that does not exist.

Why don't you go and take a long hard look down the darkest mines of yourselves? At how, in sleep and wakefulness, constellations light the hallows of your world?

From these dull panels, forged by a blue giant in red flames at an iron forge when your world was young, you cannot read your Awen: these are giants' thoughts and not for men who have given up love for old women, scrawny bald wolves, a bony haggish earth, whose minds are shrunken and empty of gods.

The breath of nine maidens will not be earned until you kiss like true lovers. So... Lleog, lay down your sword. Taliesin, cast your mind from praise poems. Arthur, be true to your bear-skin past, hear your bones and the star of the north.

Welcome fires burn at Annwn's doors for all who come in peace to my hospitality. You will feast on mead, salient boar, nine songs strummed on the harp of eternity. Yet know if you intend to kill me I have been killed a million times before.

The warm breath of maidens will turn to ice as they pursue you on raven's wings. Your stolen treasure will turn to dust. Nothing good will be brewed by the cauldron. Every blow you strike is felt in both worlds and we will be waiting when you fall.

Lleog's Flashing Sword

'Lleog's flashing sword was thrust into it,
and it was left in Lleminog's Hand...
save seven, none returned from the Mead-Feast Fort.'
The Spoils of Annwn

In the midst of the mead-feast
Lleog thrust his flashing sword
into the cauldron's mouth,
shattered its pearl-rim.

The sinking blade lit like lightning.
Reflected in it faces of a million million souls,
eyes melting, disintegrating like shadows
into pure white light.

(It reminded me of the Tower in the Tarot,
every edifice struck since,
burning towers,
falling stars,
falling souls...)

Lleminog scooped the cracked cauldron
into his hand,
escaped like a thief in the night
with moon, stars, sun, broken pieces
of Old Mother Universe jangling in his pocket.

Seven fled
the dustballs of ghosts,
haranguing teeth of red-eared hounds,
a clawed flight of ravens.

When they had slammed Annwn's gate shut
they found themselves in a world
of ruined fortresses.

They are still here now.

Diwrnach is Dead

Diwrnach is dead. He's died several times. It's not surprising in this culture obsessed with killing giants.

The great blue slabs of his limbs lie spread-eagled across the table. His fists are heavy clenched stones. His corpse is headless and his head lies in a bloody pool on the floor. His scream is frozen above his rocky beard. I dare not look into his eyes: pale, opaque, rolled into his head.

"Diwrnach is dead!" my cry resounds around the hall. There is no-one left to hear his death toll. His maids and servants were slaughtered in their beds, his courtiers drowned in blood at the table. The hearth fire is out. A circle of cinders and three deep holes mark where the cauldron stood. It's gone again: the same old tale.

I try to unravel the mystery of his death from dusty manuscripts. I trace his name: Diwrnach, Wrnach, Awarnach, Diwrnach Wyddel, Dyrnwch Gawr of the Old North; piece together the fragments into a montage. Several constants emerge: Diwrnach defended a cauldron in a feasting hall and owned a sword destined to bring his end.

The cauldron was forged at the beginning of time in Annwn's depths by a giant called Llasar Llaes Gyfnewid, 'Blue Smith who Re-forges the Weak'. Painstakingly, he enamelled its ridge and gilded it with pearls.

Its gilt iron plates told the stories of the primordial world. Its womb held the deepest reflections of Old Mother Universe: the mysteries of birth, life, death and rebirth. The Head of Annwn drew upon its wisdom. Bringing life to the dead was a power he did not possess.

When Llasar and his wife, Cymidei Cymeinfoll, decided it was time to have children they realised they must head for thisworld. The cauldron was Llasar's most prized possession. He carried it on his back through Annwn's tunnels and the pair emerged from a lake in Ireland, blue as lake-water, tossing droplets from their yellow-red manes.

King Matholwch of Ireland took them in. After a month and a fortnight, Cymidei conceived, and a month and a fortnight later birthed a fully grown armed warrior. Two months and fortnights later, another one, and so on until the rolling green hills of Ireland were thronging with giants.

The Irish disliked Llasar and Cymidei's offspring because they were large, coarse and ill-mannered. So they built an iron house, like a forge or a cauldron, then lured the family in with the promise of a feast like no other. Whilst the giants gorged themselves, they lit a fire beneath the house and fed the red flames until the plates burned white-hot.

The giants' screams crashed impotently against iron as their flesh seared and melted. Summoning all his strength, Llasar barged out with the cauldron on his back, dragging Cymidei with him. When he returned his children were little more than faceless sacks of blistering bones writhing in the relentless heat. Llasar's screams of loss and anger split the skies. His tears were a primal flood.

Llasar and Cymidei fled overseas where they were taken in by Brân the Blessed. In gratitude they gave Brân the cauldron and he allowed them to people the landscape of Prydain. They built castles in the mountains, etched their gargantuan forms into rock, made the highest summits their headlands, set out craggy chairs to watch the spiralling star-stories.

When constellations passed in the mountain lakes Llasar missed his cauldron dearly, for the images etched on its panels told the whole story of the night skies. The cauldron's absence threw Llasar into a state of melancholy. Old Mother Universe ceased to wink from the darkness. Chill words of the Head of Annwn haunted him. He thought often of his dead children.

Llasar stopped making love to Cymidei. He longed to touch only cold iron. His eyes became fixed on the horizon and his ears on the winds as he listened for news of his creation. Thus he was distraught when he heard Brân had given the cauldron to Matholwch, devastated when he heard of its misuse bringing life to dead Irishmen in thisworld.

By the time Llasar reached Ireland it was too late. The cauldron was broken. Slaughtered Britons and Irishmen lay piled around it. From the rift torn by the explosion, crept huge white hounds with red ears to take the fallen to Annwn.

Wracked by sobs, blue tears flooding down the cliffs into the Irish Sea, Llasar gathered the fragments of the cauldron into a sack, hauled it onto his back, then followed the padding hounds.

As Llasar walked through the tunnels of Annwn into the growing light he was horrified to find its green hills, woodlands, villages and castles filled with sorrowful, wrathful spirits tearing branches from trees, breaking windows, wrecking the landscape with laments, throwing themselves at the feet of the Head of Annwn, begging for rebirth.

A single look from the beleaguered ruler told Llasar what he must do. He walked to Annwn's depths. In its coldest and loneliest cavern beside a whispering stream he pieced the cauldron together part by part. At first his fingers would not work. He could not remember the patterns. His mind was as clumsy as his limbs. Then from the deep, from the spring, the Awen broke through.

The fragmentary images came together like constellations. He fired his forge. As he worked in the flames he felt the encircling presence of Nine Maidens, whose inspiration had helped him create the cauldron many centuries ago. Their breath on his neck. Their song in his ears.

However, as he heated the plates he could not shut out memories of white-hot walls closing in. The death cries of his offspring, the stench of charred flesh, the heap of blistered bodies in the iron house. He did not hear the whole song. Though he completed his forging, the images on the cauldron remained separate as constellations reflected in a mountain lake.

When Llasar turned to look for the faces of the Nine Maidens even their shadows were not there. He sank to his knees exhausted and sick with himself: the Blue Smith who Re-forges the Weak unable to complete his work because of his weakness. Water from the spring poured into the cauldron, bubbling white, echoing around the cavern with a cacophonous roar.

The Head of Annwn entered with the host of furious spirits behind him. He approached the cauldron and greeted the Nine Maidens and Old Mother Universe. "Old Mother of the Stars, I bring to you the souls awaiting rebirth." As he sang their names, not their worldly names but the soul-names they'd possessed since time's beginning, each hair on Llasar's neck rose in turn.

The spirits pressed to the edge of the cauldron, eager to catch a glimpse of their new lives, to take the plunge into the Old Mother's womb and re-enter the world down the splashing rivers of her uterus. Many went, but a small number were left with no hint of rebirth. Their screams were so terrible they turned Llasar's blue blood cold. A crippling pain gripped his heart.

Unable to see an explanation, the Head of Annwn ran his hands over the cauldron. Following the intricate grooves of its enamelled images, he felt the invisible fault-lines of the giant's doubt and pain between each story. He saw how the Old Mother's first child and his creation had been broken by the cruelty of the people of the world.

One taste of the broiling waters revealed the cauldron mirrored Old Mother Universe's broken heart and ruptured womb. Time and space fragmented. The veil between the worlds irreparably torn.

All the spirits of Annwn could no longer be reborn. A growing host would gather: those killed in battle, murdered, driven to take their own lives. It would take all his strength to prevent them from destroying the world. War was coming to both worlds and the cauldron would be safe in neither.

Llasar Llaes Gyfnewid, the Blue Smith, the only being capable of mending the cauldron, lay dead in the deepest reaches of Annwn.

The Head of Annwn called on the Nine Maidens for advice.

Nine shadows appeared on the cave walls. To the tune of a lyre:

"The Blue Smith must be reborn and named Diwrnach."

"Diwrnach must be born in a hall in every fragment of the world."

"In every fragment Diwrnach must defend the cauldron."

"Diwrnach must defend the cauldron with a sword sharper than any sword in the world."

"A sword destined to take his life."

"Diwrnach must die by his own sword."

"Diwrnach must die in every fragment of the world."

"Diwrnach must die so the world is made whole."

"But what of the cauldron?" asked the Head of Annwn. "If Diwrnach dies, who will re-forge the womb of Old Mother Universe?"

The sound of the lyre faded out. He found himself speaking to shadowless walls.

Only three stories about Diwrnach's defence of the cauldron have survived. The first is set in the Welsh mountains. Diwrnach was born to a family of giants continuously plagued by the knights of a King called Arthur who was trying to assert the reign of a Middle Eastern god who believed he was the only god and, to all accounts, looked like a bearded giant in the sky.

It was a good job Diwrnach was born full-grown and fully armed. From the moment he emerged from the womb bold, blue, fiery red and yellow-maned, he defended his people and quickly became their chief warrior and keeper of their most prized possession - a magical cauldron enamelled with wondrous images that only brewed meat for the brave.

It was rumoured that Diwrnach's prowess stemmed from the sharp-edged sword he was born with. So long as he held it the only blood that flowed down the mountain walls was the blood of knights.

One evening Diwrnach was feasting in his chieftain's seat, tearing off meat with his teeth from a pork loin boiled in the cauldron, swallowing it whole and washing it down with bragget in a tankard the size of a beer barrel, when his porter announced a man was at the door. And not just any man: a skilled man.

His name was Cai and he claimed to be the best burnisher of swords in the world. Looking down at his trusty sword, Diwrnach realised that in all his life he had not paid any attention to maintaining its legendary sharpness.

"A burnisher of swords. Just the man I need. Send him in!"

Cai was the tallest man Diwrnach had met who was not a giant; fair-haired, jovial. He handled the giant's blade with ease. Taking a striped whetstone, whistling as he worked, he polished its dark-blue edge to a white sheen thin as the horizon.

Diwrnach nodded his satisfaction. Before Cai agreed to polish the other side, he insisted Diwrnach allow his friend, Bedwyr, to come in. As Bedwyr was skilled with a spear, with a head that came off its shaft and drew blood from the wind, Diwrnach agreed.

Whilst Cai finished burnishing his sword, Bedwyr sneaked off and went about the wings of the castle slaughtering Diwrnach's maids and servants.

Cai approached Diwrnach with the sword, smiling widely, swinging it demonstratively. "It's so sharp it could draw blood from all four winds now. Bleed them dry."

"Very good." Diwrnach stood, turned and stretched his eager hands out to take his weapon.

As Diwrnach leaned close, with one swift swing, Cai sliced off his head and kicked his body back onto the table with a crash that shook the hall. Diwrnach's last scream made no sound as his head hit the floor, rolled once, twice, lay stonily still.

Uproar filled the hall. With their enchanted weapons Cai and Bedwyr made short work of the rest of the giants. When every courtier lay in pooling blood, they piled their swords, armour, jewellery and other riches into the cauldron and departed with it filled with Welsh treasure.

In Ireland, Diwrnach awoke alone and was taken in by King Odgar as his steward. Odgar gave Diwrnach a castle in the emerald hills and charge of his prized cauldron. Diwrnach defended the cauldron from all the enemies of the Irish: the Britons, the Picts, the Sidhe, with his sharp-edged sword.

Alongside Diwrnach fought an Irishman called Llenlleog who was nearly as skilled a swordsman and may have been better had he possessed Diwrnach's sword, from which he seldom removed his eyes.

One day, Diwrnach received a message from Odgar; King Arthur of Prydain was coming to Ireland and he was to give him the cauldron. Diwrnach recognised this as a trick and refused. However, the guest law of his country demanded that he must allow Arthur and his company into his hall to feast.

Although the cauldron sizzled and growled, it did not refuse meat to any of Arthur's men. Whilst the mead horn passed, Diwrnach supped bragget from his barrel-sized tankard and exchanged crude jokes about the Britons, in Irish, with Llenlleog, who sat at his right hand.

After his company had eaten and drunk their fill, Arthur asked Diwrnach to give up the cauldron. Diwrnach refused. Bedwyr seized the cauldron and put it on the back of Hygwydd, Arthur's servant. As Diwrnach rose from his seat and reached for his sword, Llenlleog snatched his sharp-edged blade and, in one swift stroke, cut off his head.

Llenlleog's blade made such quick work of the other Irishmen that Arthur and his men did not need to move from their seats. They departed with a new ally and the cauldron filled with Irish treasure.

In the Old North, Diwrnach was born to a family of giants who kept their hall in the headlands of Pennant Gofid, 'the Valley of Grief.' They lived close to a cult of witches targeted by a stream of knights coming to the valley in search of witch's blood.

The last witch was Orddu, 'the Very Black Witch.' She was adept in witchcraft and a fierce fighter. She and Diwrnach became firm friends. When Orddu's life was threatened, Diwrnach defended her with his sharp-edged sword. When Diwrnach's hall was attacked, Orddu defended it with spells, talons, her bare knuckles and wrestling skills.

One night, Diwrnach and his court were feasting. Orddu had joined them at Diwrnach's right, drinking from a tankard bigger than Diwrnach's. They were well into their cups when Arthur and his company arrived and asked for access to the hall.

"Let them in," said Orddu, "we can deal with them. Get them drunker than us and then..." She nodded toward Diwrnach's magical weapon.

As the cauldron bubbled and spat, and Arthur and his men shared meat and mead from a horn, Cai made eyes at Orddu. Orddu had a liking for tall, fair men. It was not long until Cai had ensconced himself between Orddu and Diwrnach, his hand on Orddu's thigh, then reached for Diwrnach's sword.

In one fell swoop Cai decapitated Diwrnach. With a wild scream Orddu launched herself upon Cai, grasped his sword arm and the pair fell wrestling to the floor. Whilst they struggled, Arthur and his men killed the rest of Diwrnach's court and escaped with the cauldron filled with northern treasure.

I imagine other stories existed and Diwrnach died in every one. All for the cauldron that boils meat for the brave and brings life to the dead. It's long gone now. Three holes scar the ashen ground. Its absence is enough to bring to mind bubbling water, quicken my heart.

I turn back to the fallen giant. The cold slabs of his limbs across the table, his severed head on the floor, his courtiers drowned in blood. The cauldron's deadly cost.

"Diwrnach is dead!" The Head of Annwn's voice is like a death knell. His cloak is darker than the shadows of the hall yet his eyes are bright as stars. "Diwrnach is dead: here in the mountains of Alt Clut as he is in Dal Riada, Gododdin, Rheged, Elmet, Gwynedd, Dyfed, Powys, Ceredigion, Bernicia, Deira, all the kingdoms of the Cymry, of Lloegres, of Eire, in every kingdom of the world. Yet in his death many fragments of the world have been gathered together again."

"Was this the only way?" I ask.

"There is no other way for the Nine Maidens but necessity."

"Can we at least give Diwrnach, his courtiers, his maids and servants, a proper funeral?"

"This mountain hall will be their grave. Here they will eat, drink and make merry again. Although without the cauldron they cannot be reborn... And Diwrnach, what will your fate be? Blue Smith: the only soul with the knowledge of how to re-forge the cauldron, give strength to the weak, courage to the frightened, old, old son of Old Mother Universe?"

A terrible keening grates through my bones and fills the hall. Through a chink of darkness appears an old woman:

hooded, small, bent, narrow. With a gnarled finger she points at Diwrnach's head.

The Head of Annwn sets Diwrnach's head upright and turns it to face her. The Old Mother approaches and takes a bottle of ointment from her pouch. Crooning softly, she rubs it into her oldest son's skin, bringing back the blue hue. She combs his hair with a silver comb, untangles his beard and dresses it with oil.

Once she's done, his stony eyes roll back with a staccato flash. His full colour floods back. The Blue Smith loosens his jaws...

The Last Witch of Pennant Gofid

I journeyed for weeks
through mist and hunger
to find the split rack of her bones,
bones stripped, flesh burnt
and boiled in the cauldron,
blood drained and bottled in two jars.

I plundered the ashes where the cauldron stood,
sniffed for blood where the jars were filled.
Played maracas with her bones,
made intricate arrangements,
chanted and sung
but could not raise her ghost.

"She is amongst the spirits of Annwn now,"
spoke the god I called instead.

"Lay her bones to rest. In the fire of poetry
console her burning spirit."

I'm laying her bones to rest. The Last Witch of Pennant Gofid. Her name was Orddu. It means 'the Very Black Witch'. Whether she had black skin, black hair or used black magic seems irrelevant now. All that is left is her scapula split in twain, her shattered pelvis, two arms, two legs, her broken skull. Jagged shadows in two orbits retrieved from either side of the cavern.

Her bones are still. I am angry and restless. I cannot abide the story of her death. How Arthur came as he always did into every story, every world, every myth, with his hatred of witches: sword slung over his shoulder like a sundered lightning bolt, a living knife in his hilt, a shield on his thigh adorned with an image of the Virgin Mary, aboard a huge mare.

Caw of Prydyn behind him, a giant with a curling beard; and the damned jars like heinous milk bottles on each side of his saddle, half a man in size, well-stoppered, thick-glassed, unbreakable. Then the retinue with spear and shield, tawdry banners and flags.

Following to stragglers' jeers, Hygwydd the servant staggering bow-legged, bent-backed beneath the gigantic cauldron, then Hygwydd's brother, Cacamwri, with Hir Amren and Hir Eiddil dragging ponies piled with saddle-bags of food and weapons.

At Arthur's right, Gwythyr ap Greidol, a grizzled war-lord with fire and a hundred bloody campaigns in his eyes. And to Arthur's left, Gwyn ap Nudd, the guide who tricked and dizzied their quest, cloaked in mist, summoning his hounds to eat the fallen from the mountainside.

Of the host who went to Pennant Gofid, only a fragment reached the cave where Orddu plaited her black hair, blackened her skin with war-paint, fastened down her helmet. Sharpened her sword then set it aside like an afterthought. Cracked her knuckles and flexed her talons.

When Arthur blanched, a voice mocked from the mist, "If you're scared, witch-killer, why not send in your servants instead?"

Arthur pointed Hygwydd and Cacamwri toward Orddu, who beckoned. She grabbed Hygwydd by the hair, dragged him to the floor, threw off Cacamwri's assault, arrested their weapons, beat them out bloody and bruised. Arthur sent Hir Amren and Hir Eiddil in to be crushed in her wrestling hold, torn by her talons, beaten out with broken bones. Arthur fumbled for his knife.

"Why are you afraid, Christian warlord?" Orddu asked. "Far from home. Far from heaven. Do you remember I trained your northern warriors? Without my wisdom, gifts from our gods, they would be nothing but bickering chieftains with a lust for gold and immortality that will bring Prydain's downfall."

Overcome by fury Arthur threw his knife in a wrathful arc that sliced down through Orddu's helmet, through her ribs. Dropped to the floor as she fell aside in two halves screaming, "Prydain will fall! Prydain will fall! Prydain will fall!" as the mist writhed and the hounds of Annwn howled.

When her twitching halves lay still, Caw filled the bottles with her warm blood and jammed down the corks. They stripped her of armour and flesh. Boiled a merry meal. Stole her sword. Left with a cauldron filled with northern treasure whilst her spirit watched aghast in the misty arms of Gwyn ap Nudd.

I cannot abide the story of Orddu's death. How Arthur came as he always came into every story, every world, every myth, with his hatred of witches, with his living knife, to put an end to wild, recalcitrant women. Now I've laid it to rest I'll share another story instead.

I shall tell what this fatal blow and the blows on the Witches of Caerloyw cost Prydain ("Prydain will fall! Prydain will fall! Prydain will fall!"). Not only the fall of the Old North and the Men of the North. The rise and fall of the British Empire (*it had to needed to fall*). But the splitting and bottling of magical women for over a thousand years. Draining of our blood. Boiling of our flesh. Testing if we float. Giving us *The King James Bible* and *The Malleus Maleficarum*. Taking away our prophecies and visions, gods and goddesses, our fighting strength. Confining us to virginity and chastity belts. Cutting us off from plants and spirits, rocks and rain, rivers and mist, otherworlds.

Over a thousand years on we are but shadows of ourselves. Mirrored pouts tottering on high heels. Watching ourselves on selfie-sticks. Worshipping televisions. Still split in half, bottled, boiling, floating, banging to get out.

Not long ago I split the jars. Escaped to another place. Wandered my estate kissing Himalayan balsam, watching ragwort swaying with wasps and mugwort flowering like coral. But this was not enough. Gods and fairies walked to the world of the dead and called me after. Since then I have seen the dead walk in the bright eye of the sun.

I could not go back to the jars. To glass windows and tower blocks. To numbers on computer screens. To pencil skirts of offices. To fracking rigs threatening to break both worlds.

So I came to Pennant Gofid searching for answers and companionship on my lonely path. Found only Orddu's bones and the god who took her spirit. Yet found a link in spirit with a companion and a god in the magical tradition of the Old North.

So I constructed a fire of poetry and spoke my words of consolation:

"Orddu Last Witch of Pennant Gofid
know you are not the last
to walk these paths
to caves and mountain ranges,
through otherworlds and distant ages,
seeking visions of the present,
the future and past.

The rule of Arthur has fallen.
Though Prydain still falls
we have broken the jars.
Our blood is no longer contained
by the tyrants of Arthur's court.
We are winning back our flesh,
our magic, our strength,

remembering our gods.
Know your life will be remembered
where there are prophecies and hailstorms,
rain and rivers, caves and heresy,
in the mists of Gwyn ap Nudd
where your spirit burns
forevermore."

Then I took her bones in my rucksack and crawled through to a dark chamber. On a little shelf beside Orwen, 'the Very White Witch,' I laid Orddu's bones to rest.

Efnysien's Blade

When you entered the field they trusted you,
approached shiny-eyed with pricked ears
and quivering lips,
nuzzled in your pockets for apples with warm muzzles,
didn't perceive the blade until you slit
their curious lips to the teeth,
ears to the head,
as they spun squealing
sliced their tails, their docks.

When they kicked you escaped the medley of hooves,
rose from mud covered in blood,
strangled by horsehair,
seeing crimson,
tried to cut and cut their eyelids to the bone,
gore rolling down into dark eyes
rolling white. You staggered from the field
with pockets full of horse ears filled with shouts of pain,
whiskered lips that would not be silenced.

How could you do it?
How could you hurt the horses?

Whinnies deafened your days.
Their lidless eyes never stopped watching.
The fatal consequences counted down

like hoofbeats.
You flinched on the journey to Ireland
every time a horse of sea foam
rocked the ship.

You did not escape them when your long fingers
touched the heads of men
strung up in sacks,
squeezed through bone into brain,

nor when you took your nephew
(smiling, running to his uncle),
by his ankles, spun him
round your head
and consigned him to the flames.

You could not take your eyes from the cauldron
when the dead men were thrown in,
resurrected speechless.

You knew you were dead: surrounded by horses.

They stood four-square
when you lay amongst the dead,
shaking blood from their eyes,
gnashing lipless teeth.

As you stretched out your limbs
and your cadaver jerked and sparked,

they stamped their forefeet.

The cauldron shattered:
burst the cruelty of your heart.

Amidst the fragments I found
only your bloodstained blade.

You are with the horses now,
learning how to love.

II.
Ridiculous

Dumb Man

You come mouthing words.
There are burnt out cities in your mouth.
The vocabulary of sign language
cannot convey the stories
you need to tell.
You are packed with cause and effect.
You are ticking like a bomb.
When they brought you back from the dead
why did they not give you a tongue?

The Unopened Door

"Don't open that door," Brân said before we cut off his head and brought it back from the war. We've been stuck here with it eighty years. It never speaks. Nothing happens anymore.

Life's an endless party. I drink a can every morn, with a light and breezy head look out the window where the tides ebb and roll, open another one. The days are always the same, unspiralling cigarette by cigarette.

We've got stores of food and nobody has to do any cooking. Cornflakes for breakfast and microwave meals. It's curry night every night, then there's bawdy jokes and dancing.

When we turned the music up, Brân used to sing along, but his baritone got too big for our small pop songs. When Pryderi tried to cheer him up by putting a party hat on his head, it shrivelled and fell off as he narrowed his gargantuan eyebrows.

Nothing makes him smile anymore. Not even Taliesin's rude rhymes and limericks.

We know the Awen's gone sour like the milk we cannot find, sniffing round refrigerators that never hum or leak, are never empty or grow mould.

"You'll never find it," says Manawydan, always in the background shaking his head. The one who keeps his brother's orders yet stares with longing at the sea.

There's only so much beer one can drink. Only so many games of cards and gambling chips. Only so many songs that speak of nothing but the emptiness of bliss.

My life's become a blur of repetition but for the increasing nagging in my soul.

Remember, remember, what's behind that door? There's a reason we have to keep it shut, I'm sure.

That's the point, if you remembered... but I cannot... I cannot hear my soul.

I'm getting edgy. I'm off the beer. Heart racing, clammy handed, I've got the shakes. Looking at Brân's head is beginning to make me queasy. Something within me small, trembling, winged is trying to escape.

I can't believe they're reading the same old newspapers, circling the same Monopoly board, leaving no empties where the ash trays never spill.

Manawydan's asleep on the slouchy chair dreaming of flying away as a great black seabird. He isn't going to stop me opening that door.

They're engulfed in the game. Glifau's got Regent Street and Oxford Street, but Pryderi's heading for Bond Street on double sixes. Ynog's on the edge of his seat because he's stuck in jail. Gruddieu's counting coloured notes. Something's telling me to *remember...*

Still, I slip from my seat and meander round the back of the settee. Try to look inconspicuous, like I'm stretching my legs, trying to get a better view.

That door. That door. It's a plain old thing: white painted, brass handled, just like the other ones except for the DO NOT OPEN sign Pryderi made from cardboard and string.

They haven't noticed me sliding toward it, reaching out, touching the cold, metallic handle. *Do you really want to end your time on Gwales? Remember everything that should be shut out?*

Brân's eyes flash open.

Without a doubt. I turn the handle and look out. A sea breeze whips in with plaintive cries of gulls telling of every loss we have ever suffered, every kinsman and companion lost, staccato of gun-shots, crash of bombs. The broken cauldron that birthed the Awen and split the atom.

As I look across to Prydain, in eighty years nothing has changed. They're still birthing warplanes from slick, white aerodromes and building glassy universities to teach deadly technologies. Sending young men away and bringing us back useless with headless comrades.

I remember every single thing including why I should not have opened that door. The colour fades from Brân's cheeks. The colour fades from us all. Not a year has passed. Not a thing has changed. We must face the world again and bear Brân's head with us.

The Day I Raised the Dead

The Court of the Sons of the King of Suffering was a joyless place. It is not easy living in fear of a monster. Watchmen looked out from every tower. Someone was always boiling pitch. Every door was bolted and window barred.

The people were quick-footed, furtive, slump-shouldered, gazes flickering warily or axed to the ground. Skinny dogs whined and scratched at their fleas. Even the horses looked hopeless with their cartloads of straw stuck in ruts between ghosts and cracking whips.

I lived with eight other maidens on the castle's first floor. We had a room each with a fresh linen bed, a chair, a dressing table and chamber pot. We ate in our own kitchen and in a separate room kept the cauldron where we brewed the precious ointment that raised the dead.

I'd been learning for weeks how to chop and dry comfrey leaves, prepare the flowers of camomile and calendula, infuse them into oil in glass jars that clattered in the cauldron as it bubbled, then mix the infusion with beeswax in cooking pots; yet I'd never touched a man's flesh.

The maidens had told me everything I needed to know about the King's sons. They rode off each dawn across a meadow of black and white sheep, past a tree of leaf and flame to the monster's cave. The monster hid behind a stone pillar so it could see unseen. From the pillar's shadow, brandishing a poisoned spear, it killed everyone who approached.

The King's sons were remarkably brave. Daily they faced

the shadow and what lay within it. They never spoke of the monster but it was rumoured it was born from a lake: muddy-limbed, dripping with hatred, clawed, with teeth like rusty nails and one eye that fell out of its socket.

They barely got a sword blow in before they were impaled. What magic brought their corpses back on wide-nostrilled, frothing horses was known only to the maidens who took the sons in their arms and brought them back to life.

They told me the first son has the most gorgeous freckles, the second a birth mark on his right buttock, the third is missing his little toe and the ointment can do nothing about that.

I lived my life toward my day of initiation. On the allotted hour, I carried the pots to the slab at the court gate with a tub of hot water and a sponge. As the sun set golden orange over the battlements, I listened for the groan of the portcullis and clatter of hooves on cobblestones.

The last ray winked out and a chill wind blew down my neck and lifted my skirts. The gathering crowd silenced as the gate went up and a horse of iron and thunder galloped toward me bearing the crooked corpse of a blonde young man.

I climbed the mounting block and lifted him down onto the slab, unbuckled his armour, removed his greaves, pauldron, breastplate, gauntlets, cut away his bloody undergarments. His pale, freckled skin and fine blonde hairs shone in the growing moonlight.

I washed away sweat and blood then rubbed the ointment into my hands. Beginning with the cold pads of his toes I worked upward, flexing his stiff ankles, rubbing life back into his calves, thighs, past the fur of his crotch to where I dressed his wound and anointed his chest. I cracked life into his lifeless fingers, swung his arms forward and back.

When his body was ready, I combed his hair and beard, un-tensed his face, left a drop on each eyelid and waited for him to wake. He got up, dressed in new, gleaming armour, then headed into the crowd without a word of thanks.

Before I could call him back, the second son was steam-horsed in. He was weighty, an exhaustion to lift down, strip, and raise from the dead. Buckling his armour on, he headed to the tavern without offering to buy me a drink.

I hoped the third son would be more grateful. When he sat up it looked like he desperately wanted to speak but some monster or monstrous event had tangled his tongue and left him speechless. He pulled his cloak around him and vanished with a nod.

And that was that: I'd raised the dead. I raised them every ninth day, year after year. As they were shuttled in, battered, bruised, fatally wounded, raised silent and thankless to fight again, my work began to feel futile and pointless.

Finally, I asked the other maidens why the King of Suffering knowingly sent his sons to their deaths every day.

"The King's got to keep the monster in its place."

"He's got to keep up a show of arms so the other Kings don't see his weakness."

"If it wasn't for the monster there would be no need for the King and his sons."

"And what's more... we'd be out of a job."

Whilst the other maidens continued to raise the dead unquestioningly, I began to consider running away. But where would I go knowing only one art in a land plagued by monsters?

My heart filled with hope when the cauldron stirred and in its waters we saw a knight arrive on horseback fully-armoured, visor down, hungry eyes glinting from its shadows like slits of lakes on the horizon, to slay the monster with a shining spear.

Peredur rode into the court as foreseen and watched as I raised the sons from the dead. They shook his hand and took him to feast with the King. The King laughed out loud at his plans to kill the monster. "You'll never kill it. It'll have your balls for breakfast! Once you're dead, the maidens will not bring you back to life again."

Peredur paid no heed to the King's warning. We watched in the cauldron as he rode away before dawn. On the mound outside he met a fair woman who gave him a magic stone with a mirror-like surface so he could see the monster but the monster could not see him.

He rode across the meadows of black and white sheep, past the tree of leaf and flame to the monster's cave. As he dismounted with an ominous clank the sun peeked into the reddening sky and hung in stasis, throwing a ruddy hue across the lake.

Peredur advanced toward the cave with his spear in one hand and the stone in the other. In it he saw the maw of the monster filled with nails and its eye lurching from its socket.

Before it could strike, he drove his spear into its sagging belly then cut off its head.

As its blood flowed cold as lake-water from the cave-mouth, the three sons pulled up and gaped at the knight emerging from the cave carrying its head by its matted top-knot. Peredur gave his trophy to the sons before wheeling off to slaughter a serpent for the stone in its tail.

The sons galloped back alive and displayed the monster's head on a stake at the court gate. Celebrations broke out with music, dancing, pints of ale. I didn't swing my skirts or sing because I couldn't take my eyes off that sad thing beside the slab where we'd raised the dead.

For three days the town was happy, but the King and his sons were silent and pensive. Then the sword-makers and armourers began to complain they were out of work. The townspeople questioned why they were labouring the fields to feed a court who had no use.

News soon came from the next neighbouring town that a twelve-year-old girl had disappeared. They suspected the monster from the lake the other side of the mountains. It would be coming for us soon, so the King's sons rode out again.

The cycle repeated itself until all the monsters were slaughtered and King fought against King. It was then I realised suffering would never end whilst the King ruled and I was supporting him by raising his sons.

When the other maidens were fast asleep I sneaked down

to the cauldron, lit the fire beneath it, saw what needed to be done in its bubbling depths, then made my plans.

On a muggy day at the height of war, when not only the King's sons but an army of dead men were galloped in, I threw down my sponge and upturned the pots of ointment.

The townspeople gasped in horror and the other maidens screamed.

"Killer!"

"You've left the dead for dead!"

"And about time too," I said. "They've been dead for years. What's more, they were sentenced to death the day the King sent them out to battle."

The townspeople trembled under the weight of the truth and, as predicted, turned on its speaker. I took from my purse a vial of water from the cauldron and downed it in one. Feathered arches of black wings tore from my shoulders and cracked open. My feet shrunk into claws and my body tightened into bird-form. With a black-beaked scream I flew away from the Court of the King of Suffering and broke the Spell of Nine Maidens.

Yet the death of the dead did not stop the bloodshed. Today corpses are flown in on steel horses, driven down long, wet roads to be laid on slabs in mortuaries. I no longer wish to raise them. I travel the country winged, cawing my truth and plotting the fall of the King.

Fallen Star

Where the stars have fallen they leave black holes.
This is the void I inhabit.
When a star came whistling down
it did not mean to bring destruction.
It came with a soft cry before it blew up the street.
I found it beneath the rubble.
It felt so sad and sorry for itself:
it was the only thing alive.
I keep remembering the hour of my death,
looking up at the sky,
seeing a star,
no wish,
just a blinding light.
I could have ridden a bomb down to Annwn
but I wished and wished
upon a fallen star.

Peredur's Mistake

It's been raining for weeks. Twice a day at high tide the rivers flood, washing in cans, plastic bottles, old tyres, cellophane. Effluent washes up from the drains. Some people blame global warming. Others say it's a punishment from God.

Only Peredur and I know the truth. After too many JDs he blurted out how he met the Fisher King on a rickety boat on the mill pond and was taken beneath. How knights in rusty armour taught him to fight whilst the king lay recumbent: blood, lymph and putrid ooze dripping from his wounded groin.

"That's why it stinks!" he declared, slamming his glass down on the table. "We're cursed with the legacy of an old, chthonic, dying king whilst our so-called monarchy are eating scones and supping cream tea. It's the fault of the witches, of course, for keeping him alive but failing to heal him. If only someone had the courage to finish him off."

I flinched. Tossed back the last of my vodka and swallowed my remark. He didn't mention the procession. His failure to ask the question. His lack of sympathy for his uncle and refusal to play his part. Since then he's had therapy and doesn't drink anymore.

I haven't slept for nights and can't get the stench of the Fisher King's wound off my hands. I get home at 7am. The television, hair dryer and straighteners are still working yet I'm forced to bathe in rainwater and boil it to make a cup of tea.

I put on my skirt and blouse, spray ample amounts of perfume and force my feet into my highest heels to avoid the flood. I waste another morning at the office tapping away, crooning into headphones, answering meaningless questions: the distant blonde.

At noon two lads enter, staggering beneath the weight of a heavy spear with three bloody streams pouring from its tip. A pair of women follow with a pale and waxlike head in a pool of blood on a silver plate.

Nobody turns. Nobody asks. They keep typing but have an extra cigarette at lunch break. Peredur keeps his gaze on the screen and his headphones tuned to another dimension. "No, I have no more questions." He slams down the phone and types up the case. I wipe away a single tear.

After work, rain washes over my umbrella and rises over my feet. The sewers' putrefaction is nothing in comparison to what flows from the Fisher King's wound. Knowledge that all the herbs in Britain will not cure him without Peredur's words rankles within me like that repugnant blow.

I lose the will to touch up my roots and smear foundation over the dark circles beneath my eyes. Tainted water pools on our fourth-storey. I wipe my screen. Squeeze out my headphones. Complaints increase. I repeat pre-set answers from my book. When the procession appears again my tears matter less.

After work, the mill pond has overflowed. Roads and pavements swim with dead fish. They wash up on my doorstep. As the Fisher King deteriorates I lose the ability to eat or drink.

The next morning I lift rotten fish from my desk: heavy, pregnant, laden with eggs, to suspicious whispers. When the procession enters at noon I cannot help but wail and weep.

Peredur can't turn his headphones up any louder. "Will you shut up!" he cries. "Can't you see there's work to be done? Questions to be answered. Reports to be filed. Targets to meet?"

"If you can answer all the questions," I snap "why can't you ask why this procession is recurring? Whose head is on the plate? What ails the Fisher King? If you'd asked I could have healed him. Our water would be clean and our kingdom virile. We wouldn't be trapped in office blocks, answering pointless questions, floating in the deluge of his festering wound."

Peredur tears off his headphones. His eyes are bloodshot and crazed. He curses me, "You evil witch, you loathsome hag! You and your kind are the cause of everything. I'll bet you cut off my cousin's head and put it on that bloody plate. It's your fault my uncle lingers on like your fetid, outdated beliefs. I'll be back for you once I've killed the Fisher King and every other witch in Britain!" He pulls a machete from beneath his desk then leaps through the window.

Ridiculous

'You're obliged to pretend respect for people and institutions you think absurd. You live attached in a cowardly fashion to moral and social conventions you despise, condemn, and know lack all foundation. It is that permanent contradiction between your ideas and desires and all the dead formalities and vain pretences of your civilization which makes you sad, troubled and unbalanced. In that intolerable conflict you lose all joy of life and all feeling of personality, because at every moment they suppress and restrain and check the free play of your powers. That's the poisoned and mortal wound of the civilized world.'

Octave Mirbeau

Have you ever been told your life is absurd? Ridiculous? Not quite ridiculous but a word beginning with 'se' that you can't remember, by a god?

Listen, remember.

It wasn't Gwyn, the god to whom I trusted my soul. With whom I will walk again when the bonds of thisworld break like elastic or lightning into the mist.

It was his father, Nodens. I don't remember how I got there or how he got there playing Neptune in some sea-hall.

Listen, remember.

I can't remember poems or hear the words of gods when I'm trapped in this world of papers and e-mails in this one-dimensional myopia of a room-become-an-office shrinking in with a head stuffed full of cotton wool.

Yet I can remember the mirth of Nodens' sea horses. His laughing fishes. The impossibility of living a lie in the sea. What I saw when I looked back at my life when he said the word beginning 'se'. How I wanted to laugh or scream or vomit. How I was vomited up by the sea. How ridiculous my life looked.

Listen, remember.

I can't remember poems and I can't hear the words of gods when I get up, switch on the computer, fill out forms and send polite e-mails.

When another part of myself is lost, trawling the bottomless depths for a word beginning 'se'.

It's ridiculous, isn't it?

Not the trawling. But the way I continue to live a life I know is absurd, supporting the unfair structures of establishments I do not believe in (white noise in my mind, cotton wool in my ears), not listening, not remembering, knowing it's wrong, as my truth slips away like a distant ship and I'm left in a world that is paper thin?

Listen to the poems.
Remember the voices of the gods.

Mistakes are not unchangeable and in the deep no word is lost.

III.
Drowned Lands

The Train to Drowned Lands

I. Blackpool Train

'I love the train, its sheer unstoppability'
Kim Moore

I'm on the Blackpool train sinking into that train-trance, that trance you can only sink into on a Northern Rail train. The rhythmic clippety-clop of the tracks, the hammock-lullaby sway. I forget my anxiety about going to the fracking protest. The train is no longer headed to Blackpool. It's branched right, galloped off down the track of an old Roman road. Town and coast, sky and sea are headed toward an interminable vanishing point.

II. Boddi Maes Gwyddno

'this mythology which I am possessed by'
Greg Hill

I'm possessed by a myth: 'Boddi Maes Gwyddno', 'The Drowning of Gwyddno's Lands'. This is the name of a poem in *The Black Book of Carmarthen* which formed part of a lost prose saga. Gwyddno Garanhir[4] berates his drunken gatekeeper, Seithenin, and cup-bearer, Mererid, for unleashing a flood upon his land:

> 'Stand forth, Seithenin,
> and look upon the fury of the sea;
> it has covered Maes Gwyddneu.
>
> Accursed be the maiden
> who released it after the feast;
> the fountain cup-bearer of the raging sea.'

The traditional setting of this story is Borth: an older name for Porth (G)Wyddno. The remains of a sunken forest on Borth beach suggest this may have been the location of Gwyddno's drowned land: Cantre'r Gwaelod, 'The Bottom Hundred'.

However, there are also references to 'Porth Wyddno in the North' as one of 'Three Chief Ports of the Island', Gwyddno belongs to the lineage of the Men of the North[5] and his hamper is included in the list of Thirteen Treasures 'that were in the North'. 'Boddi Maes Gwyddno' may originally have taken place in northern Britain.

4. The identity of the speaker is debatable. I do not believe it is Seithenin or Mererid as both are addressees. As the poem is titled 'Boddi Maes Gwyddno' it makes sense to me that Gwyddno speaks it.

5. Gwyddno ap Cawdraf ap Garmonion ap Dyfnawl ap Ednyfed ap Macsen Wledig.

III. Tricks of a Sunken Forest

'How many thousands of theis trees now stand
Black broken on their rootes, which once drie land
Did cover, whence turfs Neptune yeelds to showe
He did not allways to theis borders flowe.'
Richard James

I go to Rossall Point at low tide to search for the sunken forest. I cross pebbles, shells, sandy rivulets, rills, noticing knots of worms, a dead crab, football-like balls of dried eggs, to meet the sea. There are no signs of black, petrified, old trees: only a raised island occupied by herring gulls I later learn is the remains of a shipwreck.

Walking back along the promenade I notice, just a few metres away, what looks like a timber circle. Stepping closer, I recognise shiny remnants of knotty bark and whorls of cambium beneath sea weed, algae, and hordes of barnacles. I'm excited by my discovery but confused about why it isn't better known.

At Rossall Point Observation Tower I view auroch and whale bones and a collection of hamper-like 'mermaid's purses: the egg caskets of sharks and skates. A guide with a fisherman's knowledge tells me my 'timber circle' is the remains of the Rossall Point Landmark built in 1766. The sunken forest hasn't been seen for years due to rising sea levels.

IV. Portus Setantiorum

'There has been a long-held local tradition that the Portus Setantiorum, now lost to coastal erosion, was located near the mouth of the Wyre at Fleetwood.'

David Barrowclough

The location of Portus Setantiorum, the sunken harbour of the Setantii Tribe, is the subject of much speculation. The most popular view is that it lies north of Fleetwood where a Roman road was found leading out to sea. In 1920 William Ashton noted local fishermen referred to it as 'the Roman harbour' and recorded their words.

Chris Ainsworth said, 'The wall or bank goes sheer down on each side. At lowest ebb it is about 3 feet above sea level... There is a curve at the sea end, probably as protection from south-west gales, with very deep water close to the end on the north side.' Thomas Leadbetter reported 'that when his boat got aground on it the stern was on the stone bank, whilst there were many fathoms of water under the bow.'

Historian David Barrowclough notes, during the recent construction of the seawall, a harbour wall was recorded by divers '4.4m high and at least 12m long, faced with dressed stone blocks measuring 60cm square... below the surface of the sea at low tide off the coast of Fleetwood'.

The Roman road leading to this lost port and causeway joining it from Pilling Moss suggests it was of great importance. Ashton says, 'Through Portus Setantiorum would doubtless pass traffic from all parts of England to Ireland, the Isle of Man, and Manchester. It would be the "Liverpool" of the Roman period.'

Portus Setantiorum is a strong candidate for a 'Chief Port'. Its flooding would have inspired a powerful and long-lasting story. Although scholars have discredited the etymological links made by John Rhŷs between Seithenin and the Setantii, they may have a mythic basis.

V. Remarkable Earthquakes

'A bad earthquake at once destroys the oldest associations'
Charles Darwin

Roper's 'List of Most Remarkable Earthquakes in Great Britain and Ireland' records seven taking place in the 6th century. An earthquake on September 6th, 543AD, was 'General and of great extent'. In the 'British Association List of Earthquakes, 1911' Robert Mallet states this was felt 'throughout the then known world'.

A date of 543 would be entirely consistent with the period when Gwyddno, Seithenin and Mererid lived. In another poem from *The Black Book of Carmarthen*, Gwyn (a ruler of Annwn, 'the deep', also known as the Gwaelodion 'Bottoms'), converses with Gwyddno about the fall of several 6th century northern warriors. It seems possible the earthquake of 543 caused the flooding of Portus Setantiorum and drowned Gwyddno's lands.

Two statuettes dedicated to Gwyn's father, Nudd/ Nodens[6], were discovered nearby on Cockersand Moss in 1718. It has been suggested their presence indicates the proximity of a Romano-British shrine to Nodens. However, it has never been found. It seems possible it was destroyed by the flood of 543 and the statuettes were dropped by fleeing refugees.

VI. The Runaway Train

'To articulate what is past does not mean to recognize "how it really was." It means to take control of a memory, as it flashes in a moment of danger.'

Walter Benjamin

My possession by this mythology began with a vision of Gwyn and Gwyddno's conversation. Since then I've felt there's a reason these old tales are reappearing, fragment by fragment, like the sea disclosing a submerged forest.

Like in 543 and 1535 (when floodwaters swallowed Greater Singleton) sea levels are rising. In 2011 at Preese Hall, near Blackpool, the hydraulic fracturing of a horizontal well for shale gas caused two earthquakes.

6. As Mars Nodontis and Mars Donotus.

John Rhŷs suggests Mererid was originally the guardian of a Fairy Well. This is echoed by her role as 'fountain cup-bearer'. The earthquake and flood may be related to Seithenin violating Mererid. Her violation is repeated at the fracking well[7].

These stories flash their warning as man-made climate change drives the runaway train toward drowned lands. As fracking threatens to rock the earth and cause new floods they form a desperate signal to sober up, slow down, stop the train.

7. There is a Fairy Well between Staining and Hardhorn, and Preese Hall is only 3 miles away.

Pearl

Picture a drinking party on the west coast of Lancashire. Surprisingly, it's not at Blackpool where the hens are done up in feathers and L-plates and the stags are sloshing down pints at wooden tables where the tide beats in foamy gasps against the front.

This party is before the time of rainbow-coloured cocktails, plastic lips and blow-up dolls. It is a classic tale of drunkenness and fornication, the unleashing of primal forces from an oceanic pearl.

To find her, take a journey on the tram from Blackpool North to Fleetwood. On board meet our guide: Elphin, Gwyddno's son, bleary eyed, beery-breathed, shirt buttoned wrong. Like us all, he's been drinking away his sorrows. His father's rarely home. He's left the fortress to drunken Seithenin who's infatuated with a cup-bearer named Mererid, 'Pearl'.

They say she was born from a pearl
rode a bay horse up the strand
with a pearl-rimmed cup
in her hands
to quench the thirst
and test the honour of a man.

Get off at the North Euston Hotel and follow Elphin as he staggers to the mouth of the Wyre and unties a rowing boat.

Scramble in. The oars carry you beyond the ninth wave with an unsteady beat to dock at a dilapidated harbour with rotten floodgates, wide open, groaning from their hinges, and a fleet of leaky boats.

Approaching the fortress you hear the clank of glasses, a count, a glug, a slam, a rowdy song. The doorkeeper's asleep, snoring loudly, with an empty bottle in his hand.

The tables of Gwyddno's hall are lined with empties. Men and women are slung across one another like drunken rags. Seithenin's slouched on the throne, legs splayed, waving his tankard, "Where's my cup-bearer? My fountain cup-bearer? I've drunk my fill."

Mererid's the only sober one: a pearl amongst empty mussels with skin of nacre and dark, damp hair, mussel-brown. In her hands is a pearl-rimmed cup.

They say she was the guardian of a fountain:
a bottomless source
before Kings
before the Court.
If her fountain overflows
Porth Wyddno will be lost.

"Before you drink again, Seithenin," cautions Mererid, "don't you think it would be wise to close the floodgates?"

Seithenin laughs. "Open or closed, this fortress is impenetrable. For hundreds of years, no, thousands, this harbour has survived the onslaught of the sea."

"Its rulers, until now, have been wise. They have not incited the sea's rage."

"Ha! King Seithenin is the wisest of all. He has nothing to fear from the raging sea!"

"King?" Mererid laughs. "I'm not sure young Elphin or Lord Gwyddno would agree with your presumption."

"That old warlord's never here and as for his useless whelp, the only thing he's good for is catching salmon from the weir on May Day. He couldn't rule a cantref of fish!"

"How dare you," Elphin steps forward.

"Elphin!" Seithenin jumps in surprise. "And... there's four of you..." he squints. "No, two... no, four."

"Two," Elphin replies. "This is a visitor from another land and time, so stop making a fool of yourself and my family."

"Two or four all is one," says Seithenin. "All welcome. Sit yourselves down. My cup-bearer will pour you a drink once she has quenched my thirst." He thrusts his tankard toward Mererid.

Mererid shakes her head, "You have one last chance to close the floodgates." The coldness in her voice sends a wave-like shiver through the hall.

They say she held the power of the sea
in her shell like a pearl.
If cracked
she'll unfurl
nine bay horses of the waves
to drown the world.

"The floodgates will remain open," says Seithenin. Looking

Mererid up and down, "And they will not be the only gates to remain open tonight."

Mererid's eyes fill with rage. Her hair whips around her in wild bay waves. She drops the pearl-rimmed cup. As it shatters, her cup-bearer's guise breaks. In her place a fountain erupts and from it gallop nine bay water-horses.

The revellers shout and scream, attempt to rise, but fall or topple from their stools, tipping tables and shattering glasses.

As they attempt to stand the door slams open. A voice like a crane's booms, "What is this chaos in my hall?" Gwyddno Garanhir enters in battered armour, face painted black, white and red, hand-in-hand with his wife, Ystradwen.

Seithenin attempts to abort the throne, slips on the watery steps and bumps down into a groaning heap, clutching his backside beneath the fountain.

"Fool," Gwyddno curses Seithenin, "did you not realise it was never the floodgates but Mererid who stood between this fortress and the raging sea? Our bond with her is far more ancient than the lineages of the Men of the North. Because of you my northern port is ruined, my family doomed."

Thunder crashes and rain pounds the roof. Water rises to your knees. You follow Elphin, Gwyddno and Ystradwen through the downpour, down the flooded road to the harbour and climb into a leaping, bucking boat.

As Elphin rows away, you look back to see the drunkards swaying out, squabbling over leaky vessels. A bolt of lightning crashes down on the fortress, cracking and blackening the walls. Water rises to subsume Porth Wyddno. In the distance a woman watches from the back of a bay horse.

Gwyddno's Hamper

'The Hamper of Gwyddno Garanhir: food for one man would be put in it, and when it was opened, food for a hundred men would be found in it.'

The Thirteen Treasures of the Island of Britain

Gwyddno Garanhir kept a fish weir on Porth Wyddno's shores. On Calan Mai, every year, he found three hundred salmon weighing a hundred pounds. They were so rich and filled with wisdom he called them his little Bards.

Because he gave one little shimmerer back to the water, one silver thread flipping home to the source, three hundred were born and fed the hunger of a hundred men.

Thus the weir was known as Gwyddno's Hamper until foolish Elphin, Gwyddno's son, left three hundred and brought back one, the strangest of fish: a finless, flipperless, shining browed Bard, aquatic eyed, translucent skinned, with a voice like a dolphin promising luck and plentiful songs.

When a billow of cranes flew overhead with trumpety, creaky calls, from the alphabet of their legs Gwyddno read of Elphin's liberation by his silver-tongued Bard, ships arriving to bear the strange fish north, his high and eerie voice singing the deathsongs of fallen warlords.

A hundred plates went empty at Porth Wyddno that night. A hundred bellies groaned. Three hundred fish slipped into the unknown. When Gwyddno opened his hamper the next year all he found was fish-bones.

The Crossing of Gwyddno Garanhir

Mist drowns the beach at Borth. Not this-Borth or the other-Borth but somewhere inbetween. An old man, grey-skinned, crane-legged, picks his way along the pebbled edge of his drowned land, spumes of tidal foam spilling over his feet.

He recalls days of watching cranes from the estuary: wide white winged, red and black masked, knowing every step of their dancing legs and its meaning. Words and letters are now slipping away like the patterns of that intricate black-legged dance.

Images wash against him: a drunken sloth, a dishevelled maid, between them a broken cup. Open floodgates and the sea washing in, scarred by lightning bolts beneath a sky of storm.

The madness of a leaping coracle. A face white as sea-foam. A cold hand sliding from his grasp as with a swirl of blonde she was gone.

A youth stirring a cauldron spilling three careless drops. Cracking black iron. A deluge of poison. His beloved horses drinking, rolling, burning, searing, tossing their necks, lips spuming froth.

His son finding that youth sewn into a weathered crane-skin bag instead of salmon in the abundant weir. Unpicking the stitches. The flashing needle speaking its letters. The immortal speech of the radiant-browed one stepping uncanny from the dark unfolding womb.

How that child-bard freed his son from the dragon's castle. His grey-eyed worry and irregular beating of his heart.

The old man can no longer remember any names. He believes this is because the cranes are gone. They upped on white wings on the day of the storm, dark legs carving ominous signs across the skies. Settled in new wetlands. Visited estuaries until the poison spilled, their trembling legs gave way and their wings sunk under the boiling muddy brew (as his wife sunk years before).

He will never see each red and black face he knew by name. She will never don her mask. They will never dance, elegant and long-legged at court or knee-deep wading through wetlands.

He will never match faces to names. He will never remember his kinsmen who died fighting in the north as he lay in his chamber afloat on despair and old age, lifted only by imagined cries of cranes returning. He can no longer remember his name.

He picks his way along the edge of his drowned land, white tidal spumes tugging at his feet, face grey and weathered like a bag of crane-skin on tall and unsteady legs. His twitching shoulders remind him of wings carrying him to this beach where he drowns in mist and nameless sorrow.

Beginning to fear he cannot bear his sadness anymore he looks west. The sky is lit by a mysterious brightness. Breaking the pall a white warrior steps from the mist with a horned helmet, upright shield and spear, leading a white horse streaming from its bridle and a white dog with a tail of clouds whose red nose is the setting sun.

In his gaze the old man sees a million battles: shattered shields, broken helmets, heads pierced by spears. His ears fill with battle-cries. Death-cries.

He sways in awe and terror before the fierce bull of battle, who seems to carry the dead within his person, yet addresses him in the traditional manner and asks with dignity for protection.

"You who ask shall have protection." The warrior's kindness is disarming.

The old man trembles with relief. "Who are you? Where do you come from?"

"I come from many battles. Many deaths."

Death scenes flash before the old man's eyes. Blood-drenched armour. Men bent on spears. Words wrenched from agony. Flesh torn by ravens. He sees faces but cannot remember their names, although he shares their pain and tears drench his cheeks. A wild whinny shakes him.

"My horse is Carngrwn from battle throng," says the warrior. "My name is Gwyn ap Nudd, lover of Creiddylad, daughter of Lludd."

When the old man hears those names his inner crane-knowing awakens. He remembers his mother's stories about Gwyn ap Nudd: the warrior-huntsman who haunts wildernesses and places of the dead and may be invoked or placated for love of his partner. He remembers her crane-tales. How she lifted him from a crane-bag and gifted him with a name.

“My name is... garan...” he stumbles in reply... “Gwyddno... Garanhir.” As he recalls being taken into his mother’s white, feathery wings, other memories flood back to him: the names of his wife Ystradwen, his son Elphin, the child-bard Taliesin, Seithenin and Mererid who unleashed the flood.

Gwyddno speaks his rush of memories to Gwyn, who listens patiently until Carngrwn paws the tides and pulls away from the bridle, chomping foam from his golden bit.

“The white horse calls this talk to an end,” Gwyn speaks abruptly. “We must depart to further bloodshed in Tawe and Neath, not this Tawe but the one far away where the tide ebbs fiercely on the shore. To my sorrow I attended a battle at Caer Vandwy...”

Gwyddno shivers at Gwyn’s words of another Tawe and the name of a fortress that is not of thisworld. He recalls stories about Gwyn riding forth from the otherworld to gather the souls of the dead. An awful knowing washes over him, like tidal waters, beginning from his toes.

The white hound draws closer, ruddy-nosed. “His name is Dormach,” says Gwyn. “Do not fear him. He was with Maelgwn and has accompanied many of the men of your lineage to protection within my realm.”

Gwyddno’s vision swims. Dormach shifts into mist to dog again, his nose to sun to nose. The death-hound’s gaze remains constant, inescapable.

“I was there at the deaths of Gwenddolau son of Ceidio,” Gwyn says, “Bran son of Ywerydd, Llachau son of Arthur, Meurig son of Careian and Gwallog son of Llenog. I helped them cross. They will be waiting for you on the otherside.”

As the names of long forgotten kinsmen return to match their war-torn faces, Gwyddno yearns to be re-united. His crane-wings stir.

Yet the gatherer of souls has not finished his speech. Gwyn cries:

"I was there when the warriors of Prydain were slain,
from the east to the north;
I live on; they are in the grave.

I was there when the warriors of Prydain were slain,
from the east to the south;
I live on; they are dead."

Gwyn mounts his rearing white horse and they depart in a fury of sea foam into clouds of unendurable brightness.

The mist lifts and Gwyddno sees his lost land illuminated within a boat's reach by the light of the setting sun. Yet he does not need a boat and oars to follow where Dormach leads.

Gwyddno Garanhir hears the call of cranes bellowing, aching, sees their white wings, recognises every face, knows it is time to return to the flock. He spreads his wings. Puts on his red-black mask. His legs spell his crossing in black letters across blue-bright skies as he joins his kindred, finally touching feathers with his wife, promising later they will dance their names.

IV.
Operation Cauldron

Sea Raven

"Why do you want me to be perfect?"

It's a difficult question to ask my mother when she's laid up in hospital again, heavily pregnant, exhausted from the court case.

There's been another disaster at the chemical plant, three people injured, one missing presumed dead. That young man's name was Gwion Bach. He was employed in the control room in charge of the 30,000 gallon reactor vessel. His task was to keep the paddle stirring at several thousand revolutions a minute and monitor the changes in heat and pressure.

He was an absentminded sort, so lost in daydreams he didn't realise the paddle had stuck. The temperature rose over 300°F. By the time he'd filled the cooling jacket it was too late. With a sound like a jet engine and deafening crash, the reactor exploded with a blast that broke every window.

Gwion was seen staggering from the control room like a drunk toward the toxic brew, dipping his finger in and putting it to his lips, his hair standing on end, before my wrathful mother leapt from the offices and he hare-footed it away with her hot on his heels.

She's been cleared of murder on lack of evidence. Who would believe the truth: that she chased him down, swallowed him whole and he's now gestating in her womb?

The judges were far more interested in the 365 compounds she used this year, their legality and whether adequate attention had been paid to health and safety.

She got off scot free... as ever. She's a scientific genius with a meticulous eye for detail. Everything was blamed on Gwion's negligence.

We managed to minimise the damage by containing the overspill. Residents were advised not to drink from the taps for seventy-two hours and to bring their grazing animals in from surrounding fields.

I'm becoming an expert in hazard control, yet it riles me that my mother continues to make these mistakes for the same reason. After all these centuries she still can't look at my face.

She can't abide ugliness: the dark hairs on my cheeks, my swarthy skin, over-bearing belly, webbed feet and trailing wings.

I was born with the name Morfran, 'Sea Raven'. I grew up gawky as a cormorant. When I failed to shed my black feathers and gawkishness she called me Afagddu, 'Utter Darkness.'

She wanted me to be a knight but I was unacceptable to Arthur's court, unlike my sister, Creirwy, 'Lively Darling' who slipped with ease into a lacy gown and joined the gossip of the fair maidens.

That's when mother started making the potions to 'cure' me. I was glad when her first idiot apprentice broke the cauldron even though it flooded Bala and poisoned the rivers. I hoped the stinking, rotten fish, birds falling from the air, carcasses of horses and sheep and vegetationless estuaries would teach her the error of her ways.

But, as the years have passed, scientific advances have only made her more determined. She's set up a chemical plant in my name. She wants me suave, clean-shaven, the head of the company in a priceless suit with ironed-in creases.

Right now she's apologising for me to the nurses. I'm an embarrassment, a failure, unlike Creirwy who's a WAG and appeared on the front of last month's Cosmopolitan.

All I'm good at is fishing and clearing up dirty streams. I'd better go and swallow more stones...

She still hasn't answered my question.

Perhaps that's where I'll go: down to the deep where there is no ugliness and no perfection, surface with a fish for a clean breath of air before her child is born and the cycle begins again.

Under a Green Sea

'Dim, through the misty panes and thick green light,
As under a green sea, I saw him drowning.'
Wilfred Owen

After Ypres[8], Arthur commanded me to take the cauldron to Porton Down. He summoned his advisers and told them of the greenish-yellow cloud, the soldiers of Prydain blinded, choking, collapsing and burying their faces in the mud as foam gargled from their lungs.

"Chlorine, phosgene, adamsite, lewisite, tear gas, mustard gas, you will brew and put to the test. The safety of Prydain is in your hands."

They set up the animal farm and advertised for volunteers for experiments with the Common Cold. The servicemen arrived expecting a runny nose, sniffles and a sore throat. Not an inner drowning of the lungs.

For King and Country, I bore the cauldron whilst Arthur's advisers listened to wheezing chests and throats of phlegm; counted blisters; bandaged weeping, reddened skin. I fought off green waves of nausea as it buckled my knees and wore a hollow in my spine.

When I heard an old woman's lament, I repeated my mantra, plugged my ears as she screamed while the soldiers of

8. On 22 April, 1915, near the Belgian town of Ypres, German military engineers released 160 tons of liquid chlorine, enveloping tens of thousands of Allied soldiers. 5,000 were killed on the battlefield and 10,000 wounded.

Prydain unleashed poisonous gases at Loos and the Somme and foreign men drowned in yellow-green seas.

After the Armistice, when Arthur signed 'The Protocol for the Prohibition of the Use in War of Asphyxiating, Poisonous or other Gases, and of Bacteriological Methods of Warfare', I near collapsed in relief. I dared hope my task was at an end, that I could return to ironing Arthur's trousers, polishing his shoes...

Yet war broke out again and Arthur learned the enemy were stockpiling deadly nerve gases: sarin, tuban, soman. They re-lit the cauldron, re-opened the gas chambers. I heard men screaming, saw them crawling out, pumped full of atropine[9], hooked up to iron lungs.

I'll never forget the young man who, after two drops of sarin had been dripped onto his forearm, said, "I'm feeling pretty queer" then collapsed into convulsions, vomited frog spawn, turned blue. No remedy could save him from the worst case of nerve gas poisoning in the Western world.

"For King and Country"... "For King and C..." I choked and nearly regurgitated my words. I sank to my knees, trembling beneath the cauldron, shaking, sobbing, green with guilt.

For many years after the war I bore my burden through the suffering, the lies, the cover-ups. As the stories are revealed I wonder how long it will take them to find me; cowering beneath an iron weight, drowning under a green sea.

9. A medication used to treat nerve agent poisoning.

Operation Cauldron

'Have you built your ship of death, O have you?'
D. H. Lawrence

I wake in the night and see the vessel hanging in the cabin of the Ben Lomond. It clanks and clanks as waves rock the ship, ringing like a death-knell through plague-soaked mists.

Pathetic squeaks of small things dying run through my ears on pink, scampering feet. I'm amongst monkeys screaming, strangling themselves in their cages, as the knell bangs out: Operation Cauldron.

This is not the work of my mother's misguided kindness, her quest to gift with perfection her ugly son. It is the doing of those who stole the cauldron and in its broken womb are brewing war.

I fly from my bed of reeds and seaweed on sleek, black wings slicking north. I follow the cries of gulls passing on the tale from beak to ear in foghorn voices, until I reach the Isle of Lewis.

Beside obdurate cliffs, HMS Ben Lomond is anchored fast. On a nearby pontoon, men in white safety suits and gas masks load boxes of squealing guinea pigs and struggling monkeys onto the deck, turn their faces into the wind.

The men go below then a boom swings out, a bomb on the end like a dark and sinister apple. It launches and bursts. From its poisoned core showers a cloud more deadly than the dew of the witches of Annwn.

The skies fill with screams and tears. The men reappear in a white and plastic stream, take the infected animals into the hold, then bring up more boxes ready for the next round.

There's little I can do but go below, an ugly man, like a ghost, in black feathers, comforting the dying. Guiding the dead back to the old guinea pigs, the old monkeys, back to my mother's womb.

Inbetween times I rifle through the papers, read about the pathogens: brucellosis, tularemia, pneumonic plague, bubonic plague, shipped from Porton Down.

I visit the laboratory where one hundred guinea pigs are autopsied in an hour; bodies spinning on a carousel, labelled, sliced open, snips of spleen and lymph nodes collected on a plastic dish, pathology reported and written down.

Corpses are thrown away like soft, white toys into the incinerator. I tend the unacknowledged funeral. The men in white suits shy from the bird-shaped shadow cast by death-eating flames. They run from the deck when I overshadow them, nostrils filled with the scent of burning flesh.

On the last day of Operation Cauldron they launch the last bomb. I'm the first to see the Carella, a trawler approaching from Fleetwood. When Ben Lomond's crew see her, they wave warning flags and flash signal lamps like frenzied will-o-wisps. She sails like a blind woman into the bubonic plague cloud.

"Black death!" "Black death!" "We could have infected fellow humans with black death!" panicked whispers spread amongst Ben Lomond's crew.

They ring the Admiralty and are told, "Do not stop them:

secrecy is paramount. We will send a ship to track them, prevent them from docking or making contact with other vessels. If they signal for help we'll send in a medical team with injections of streptomycin[10]."

I follow the plague-ship from the Isle of Lewis, northward bound, battling through icy winds beyond the Faroe Isles. I watch the crew for weakness, fever, muscle cramps, vomiting, black swollen lymph nodes. They look at me as if I'm a dark angel or albatross but fear me less than the ghost-ship following just out of sight on the horizon.

Frost rimes the deck as they reach the fishing grounds and cast their nets. Working from dawn until the Northern Lights flash, they haul in net-loads of fish, stack them in crates. They get used to my presence on the mast and feed me crumbs of sea-biscuits (they don't see me stealing fish!).

They're tired, weak, grey-faced, by the time they have filled the hold. Shivering in sou'westers, no feeling in their extremities, they cast off and sail for warmer climes. Throughout their long journey the strange cormorant with his gaudy bill and primitive neck makes them smile. They laugh when he spreads his black wings and poses like a trapeze artist on the rigging. At last, they reach Fleetwood and return to the arms of their loved ones.

Fifty years later, the truth about Operation Cauldron is revealed and the Carella's crew learn how narrowly they escaped death. Some thank God and some thank the cormorant, scattering crumbs of sea-biscuits on Fleetwood beach.

10. An antidote for plague.

Stairway to the Stars

Did I ever tell you
about the Stairway to the Stars?

Days and nights in a hospital bed?
Walls moving in and out

to the rhythm of my breath?
How I gripped the drowning covers,

sank in a sea of sweat as the world melted?
Faces dripped away like masks?

At the end of my bed was a gateway
from which soldiers stepped.

My brother, Charlie,
sat beside me and rolled a cigarette.

We reminisced about our train-set,
girls with big smiles and long legs.

Other men limped from the trenches,
recounted their losses,

advised not to tell my interrogators.
I kept my mouth damn shut.

One day I slipped away
off the end of my bed and they took me

to see the Stairway to the Stars:
a diamond spiral rising like a Slinky into the heavens.

Upon it soldiers trod with tattered boots,
bleeding sides,

holes in the head.
When they came back down they realised

it was all a lie.
There's no reward for good soldiers.

There's only us and him;
the one dressed like a military commander

who embraces us when we descend,
like a father,

with his red-eared hounds takes us
back to our sisters, mothers,

lovers we never had.
Oh the lies, my son!

Never join the army.
Never trust the lies of Porton Down.

V.
Uranium

Silent Springfields

I didn't know it was there. Several months ago I visited Lund Church in Clifton, Lancashire. Photographing the stone cross in front of the railings surrounding the site, I never questioned what lay behind. I never asked. Springfields concealed itself in the mist like an Annuvian fortress.

Ask the right questions and you get surprising answers. Since the protests against fracking I've been educating myself on the UK's energy industry. I asked "Where does nuclear power begin?"

The answer astounded me. It begins at Springfields, just outside Preston, within cycling distance of my house. Springfields produces most of the fuel for the UK's reactors.

And nuclear power began there. The plant produced the first uranium billet and the fuel for the world's first commercial nuclear power station at Calder Hall (modern-day Sellafield), in Cumbria, which started generating in 1956.

Fuel production begins with the arrival of canisters of uranium hexafluoride. Uncannily, this is nicknamed 'hex'. Hex is converted into uranium dioxide powder by 'mixing it with steam and hydrogen in a kiln' before it is processed, pressed, heated in a furnace and ground to produce thimble-sized fuel pellets.

For Advanced Gas Reactors the pellets are 'stacked inside a stainless steel fuel tube' then 'put together in the graphite sleeve to form the fuel assembly'. For Light Water Reactors they are loaded inside three metres-long zirconium alloy tubes and fitted inside a pre-assembled framework.

Springfields also recovers uranium from a range of materials and offers 'sampling, material sorting, size-reductions, re-canning and re-drumming'. These processes take place in the Enriched Uranium Residue Recovery Plant, Nitric Acid Wash Facility, Natural and Depleted Uranium Recovery Plant, Obsolete Cylinder Wash, Uranium Hexafluoride Cylinder Wash, Enriched Decontamination Facility and Natural Decontamination Facility.

Springfields manufactures hex!

Uranium trioxide is converted to uranium tetrafluoride through hydration with nitric and sulphuric acids and reduction in a 'hot rotating kiln'. The Hex Plant then converts uranium tetrafluoride to uranium hexafluoride through reaction with 'elemental gaseous fluorine in a fluidised bed reactor at 475°C'. It is filtered, condensed, then run off as a liquid to the Hex Filling Station.

This information, from the Springfields website, has provided some insight into what goes on in its impenetrable white buildings with their silver steaming chimneys. It all seems transparent. Yet the radioactivity of uranium, coupled with chemical reactions, is troubling and raises concerns about the impact on the local environment.

Springfields takes its name from springs in nearby fields running into Deepdale Brook, which flows through the midst of the site into the Ribble. This seems like a hazard alone. A web search turned up a shocking piece called 'The River Ribble - Birthing the Nuclear Nightmare' by Marianne WildArt.

Marianne cites articles in the *Lancashire Evening Post* from 1991. Friends of the Earth measured the radiation levels from where the Springfields discharge pipe empties into the Ribble at four points upstream: 'the Cadet Hut at Penwortham Bridge, Broadgate, Penwortham Lower park and the mainline railway bridge' (all a short distance from my house) and found 'doses of radioactive thorium particles... six times higher than normal.'

If a child played on the river bank for 80 minutes a day for a year they would receive 'the maximum tolerable radiation dose of 100 units'. I frequently walk by the Ribble, descend onto its banks, and have collected stones (I keep several in my bedroom) and river water. I had no idea the Ribble was radioactive.

The survey coincided with the screening of a Granada TV programme investigating Springfields' radiation safety standards. This was based on the claims of Joe McMaster, who worked there for 31 years as an analytical chemist, that 'three of his daughters died between 1958 and 1987 from illnesses linked to fatal doses of radiation'. It's notable the Springfields Nuclear Fuels Laboratories were closed in the 1990s and are being decommissioned. A look at Springfields' most recent environmental report shows that waste products are still being discharged into the Ribble and the atmosphere.[11]

As the first generation of the UK's nuclear power stations reach the end of their life-spans, plans are being made to build a second generation. One of these will be located at

11. The most concerning are nitrate 455,210kg, uranium 0.56GBq and nitrous oxides 102,934kg.

Moorside, eight miles north of Sellafield. With three AP1000 two-loop pressurised water reactors generating 1133MW each, it will be the biggest in Europe.

The plans for Moorside have generated opposition. The history of nuclear energy at Sellafield is fraught with controversy. The Windscale fire of 1956 released radioactive material across the UK and Europe and has been linked to an increase in childhood leukaemia.

During the Miners' Strike of 1974 waste fuel overwhelmed the lines and stayed in the storage pond too long. The rod coverings corroded, then the exposed fuel reacted with the water, forming a layer of radioactive sludge. This is only now being pumped off to allow a clean-up of the hazardous pond.

NuGen, the UK energy company planning to build Moorside, are partners with Toshiba. Worryingly 'Toshiba supplied the steam generator, architecture and reactor for Fukushima reactors numbers 3 and 5, while Hitachi (merged with Toshiba) supplied the reactor, steam generator and architecture for Fukushima reactor no 4.' Toshiba also owns 60% of Springfields.

If the plans for Moorside go ahead it looks like Silent Springfields, under the radar, near invisible as radiation, could be surreptitiously converting uranium into nuclear fuel just outside Preston for a long, long time.

Cherenkov Blue

'Hygwydd, Arthur's servant...
His duty was always to carry Arthur's cauldron.'
Culhwch and Olwen

The lake's Cherenkov blue.
The rods are spent but so alive.
Knowing they will outlive me
brings pain and promise.

I could stand here for millennia
counting down how long atoms
take to decay. I could wait
until the end of the universe

if I was not decaying. If the
unstable concrete was not melting.
If it was not for these cracks
interceded by weeds,

gulls playing in radioactivity.
The risk of blue waters exceeding the vessel.
It has burst so many times
it is time to step in,

not to sink or swim but send in submarines,
embrace subaquatic intelligence.
We have cleared milky water,
siphoned off the sludge,

stored it up in steely canisters
for the next stage.
Who will become
the cauldron-bearer after me?

Uranium

'I was in a multitude of forms
before I was unfettered:
I was a slender mottled sword
made from the hand.
I was a droplet in the air.
I was the stellar radiance of stars.'
'The Battle of the Trees'

It comes from the stars. It was born from supernovae. A star goes supernova when it has burnt up all its fuel and its core implodes. This creates an explosion throwing out heavy metals whilst the star shines ten billion times brighter than it has ever shone before.

Since the earth formed, the radioactive decay of uranium has driven its convection. Uranium is a shapeshifter, naturally decaying through 14 different forms[12]. It has shaped the earth and continues to shape the fate of humanity.

Uranium decays because of its atomic structure. With 92 protons in its nucleus it is too big for itself. Its 'centre' literally 'will not hold'. Therefore it casts off protons and neutrons, losing mass, shifting shape, generating energy.

The discovery of the radioactive decay of uranium was followed by nuclear fission: bombarding a uranium nucleus with a beam of neutrons causes it to split, releasing neutrons that

12. Thorium-234, protactinium-234, uranium-234, thorium-230, radium- 226, radon-222, polonium-218, lead-214, bismuth-214, polonium-214, lead-210, bismuth-210, polonium-210, lead-206.

hit other nuclei in a chain reaction.[13] The potential was recognised to generate vast amounts of energy leading to the development of nuclear power and the nuclear bomb.

I thought nuclear fission was manmade until I read about 17 natural nuclear reactors in Oklo, Gabon, Africa, which were active 2.5 billion years ago, when simple bacteria in the oceans were beginning to respire.

3.7% of the uranium there was U-235: the perfect amount to sustain nuclear fission. Oklo's deposits lay beneath sandstone and granite. Underground water acted as a neutron moderator and made the nuclear chain reaction possible.

Heat changed the water to steam, which calmed the reaction. Once the water had condensed, the reaction recommenced. The cycle repeated every three hours and continued for hundreds of thousands of years until the fissile materials ran out.

The existence of the Gabon reactors has been used by scientists to advance arguments for nuclear power and our capacity to store nuclear waste safely underground.

This discovery was significant: two years ago Gwyn showed me a cauldron filled with stars. Since then I've been trying to make sense of it by tracing the story of the cauldron from the ancient British myths where it represents the womb of Ceridwen, Old Mother Universe, through to modernity.

13. 2 creates 4, 4 creates 8, 8 creates 64, 64 creates 4,096, and so on

I was therefore amazed to find 17 cauldrons filled with starry uranium in Oklo's underworld. Two billion years ago, Old Mother Universe was performing nuclear fission of her own accord! This has led me to ponder whether the roots of our myths are far older than we thought.

In these 17 star cauldrons we find Ceridwen performing her magic perfectly before she births her beautiful daughter and ugly son. As she stirs her cauldron, life breathes into existence. The long trail of shifting shapes leading to the origin of humanity begins.

2.5 billion years later, in the British Isles, Ceridwen puts her young human apprentice, Gwion Bach, in charge of her cauldron and everything goes wrong. On the final day of brewing a potion that will rid her son, Afagddu, of his ugliness, Gwion spills three drops.

These three drops represent the Awen which is depicted as three dots emanating three rays. This gives him the ability to shapeshift. Uranium also emits three rays: alpha, beta and gamma, and causes transmutations. This story has 2.5 billion year old roots *and* relates to the effects of radiation in the here-and-now.

Gwion flees in the form of a hare, fish, and bird before transforming into a grain of wheat and being eaten by Ceridwen. He is then reborn from Ceridwen's womb as Taliesin, knowing all the mysteries of Old Mother Universe.

A consequence of Gwion's reception of the Awen is that the cauldron shatters and poisons the land and its inhabitants. This disaster, first set at Bala in Wales, repeats itself at Windscale, Chernobyl and Fukushima.

Acquiring uranium to fill our nuclear reactors is also dangerous and damaging. Mining has existed nearly as long as mankind, but only since the 19th century have we hacked, drilled and blasted precious metals and minerals from underground on an industrial scale.

This is represented in the 'The Spoils of Annwn' where Taliesin, Arthur and his men plunder the underworld for the star-filled cauldron of the Head of Annwn. The theft is completed in one lightning-like move when Lleog thrusts his flashing sword into the cauldron.

Hauntingly, this image also evokes the penetration of a nucleus by a beam of neutrons and the rod shot into the cauldron-like receptacle in a uranium bomb. Its flash of light anticipates the blinding brightness of a nuclear explosion.

Uranium was mined in Cornwall between 1889 and 1900 and now exists only in sub-economic quantities in Britain. Hence we ravage the underworlds of other continents instead.

By 1997, 16 of the natural fission reactors in Oklo had been mined away by the French. Only one was left, in Bangombé, 30 kilometres south-east of Oklo. Scientist Francois Gauthier-Lafaye wrote a plea to Nature asking for the mining to be stopped:

'The last known natural fission reactor on Earth is likely to be mined this year. Because these natural reactors are unique, at least one should be preserved for present and future research programs... This deposit will be completely mined out soon, in 1998... We propose that this unique, scientifically important deposit be preserved for present and future research. This deposit is no less unique, and certainly more irreplaceable, than the most valued specimens from the Moon and Mars.'

I've found no evidence the last natural reactor in Bangombé was saved. We've done away with the wisdom of Old Mother Universe and assaulted the fortress of the Head of Annwn. To whom will we turn when we want to bury our nuclear waste? When disaster strikes, to whom will we run?

Warning Sign

What will represent the burial of dead stars?
What will represent the poison
and its effects?

They suggest a triune black fan
(three blades of Awen gone wrong),
Edward Munch's 'The Scream',
hands clasped to a yellow
alienesque head.

In Kakadu aborigines etched
the sickness: hands clasped
to an orange face,
knotty swollen joints,
where we mine our uranium.

Who will heed a warning sign

when we've lost our dreamtime,
songlines, stories?

When no signs have meaning?

When all is left is hunger
for dead stars?

After the Meltdown

After the meltdown life returned. Mosses greened over blackened fence-posts. Shoots broke through barren soil: jagged leaves of dandelion, willowherb shedding seeds from pink flowers, ragwort, dock, bird's foot trefoil. With them came mites, insects, spiders weaving tensile dewy webs, spittlebugs frothing stems.

Then nibbling field mice and dark-eyed voles built nests beneath the meadows and changing skies, birthing litter after litter, pink and quick-pulsed. Scurrying feet shifting stems in trailing lines caught hawk-eyes, brought owls flying low at dusk and sprinting foxes.

A herd of horses cantered free across the fields and fells, drank from streams and rivers to which fish and pearl mussels returned. Sheep grazed the hillside, growing more populous than stones.

Beneath the shadow of the sarcophagus an old woman walked with her basket, collecting herbs. She picked mugwort, meadowsweet, yarrow, nonchalantly entered the concrete tomb to scrape off swathes of black, velvety, melanin-rich fungi from around the broken reactor, humming a strange old tune.

When her basket was full of radiotropic delicacies she walked past abandoned farms, a flowering combine harvester, to the seaside town. Ivies and honeysuckles climbed walls.

Buddleia and wildflowers exploded in gardens. Birds nested in every rafter: starlings, swallows, housemartins, even the black-headed and black-backed gulls.

In a cottage close to the sea she laid out her herbs to dry on a board beside a cracked and rusty cauldron. As the kettle boiled on a portable stove she took down a jar of camomile, exchanged her sandals for slippers, crooned at her slinky, stretching cat. She poured her brew and sank into a rocking chair beside the window.

As the sun set over the sea, warming her wrinkled skin and dappling the waves orangey-red, she felt at peace. Then she saw the cormorant flying black and sleek toward the shore. Her eye turned to the cauldron, the giant's head in the corner of the room, but she was too tired to move.

Dusk fell. She heard the hoot of an owl, the howling of wolves, or was it finally the Hounds of Annwn?

Looking out into the starlit night she recalled explosion after explosion, the faces of her beautiful daughter and ugly son, the bang with which the universe began. Her eyes grew heavy and she fell asleep.

Bibliography

Introduction

Kristoffer Hughes, *From the Cauldron Born*, (Llywellyn, 2013)

The Star Cauldron

William F. Skene (transl.), '*The Spoils of Annwn*', *The Four Ancient Books of Wales*, (Forgotten Books 2007)

The Star-Strewn Pathway

Wirt Sikes, British Goblins, (General Books, 2012)

The Broken Cauldron

Charlotte Guest (transl.), '*The Story of Taliesin*', *The Mabinogion*, (Digireads, 2010)

William F. Skene (transl.), *The Book of Taliesin, The Four Ancient Books of Wales*, (Forgotten Books 2007)

The Head of Annwn Addresses Arthur's Raiding Party

Marged Haycock (transl.), '*Preiddu Annwn*', *Legendary Poems from the Book of Taliesin*, (CMCS, 2007)

Lleog's Flashing Sword

Caitlin and John Matthews, *King Arthur's Raid on the Underworld* (Gothic Image, 2008)

Marged Haycock (transl.), *'Preiddu Annwn'*, *Legendary Poems from the Book of Taliesin*, (CMCS, 2007)

Diwrnach is Dead

Caitlin and John Matthews, *King Arthur's Raid on the Underworld* (Gothic Image, 2008)

Charlotte Hussey, *Glossing the Spoils*, (Awen Publications, 2012)

Marged Haycock (transl.), *'Preiddu Annwn'*, *Legendary Poems from the Book of Taliesin*, (CMCS, 2007)

Rachel Bromwich (ed.), *The Triads of the Island of Britain*, (University of Wales Press, 2014)

Sioned Davies (transl.), *'The Second Branch' and 'Culhwch* and *Olwen'*, *The Mabinogion*, (Oxford University Press, 2007)

William F. Skene (transl), *'Pa Gur'*, *The Four Ancient Books of Wales*, (Forgotten Books 2007)

The Last Witch of Pennant Gofid

Sioned Davies (transl.), *'Culhwch and Olwen'*, *The Mabinogion*, (Oxford University Press, 2007)

Efnysien's Blade

Sioned Davies (transl.), *'The Second Branch'*, *The Mabinogion*, (Oxford University Press, 2007)

The Unopened Door

Sioned Davies (transl.), *'The Second Branch'*, *The Mabinogion*, (Oxford University Press, 2007)

The Day I Raised the Dead

Sioned Davies (transl.), *'Peredur'*, *The Mabinogion*, (Oxford University Press, 2007)

Peredur's Mistake

Sioned Davies (transl.), *'Peredur'*, *The Mabinogion*, (Oxford University Press, 2007)

Ridiculous

Octave Mirbeau, *Torture Garden*, (Createspace, 1989)

The Train to Drowned Lands

David Barrowclough, *Prehistoric Lancashire*, (The History Press, 2008)

Charles Darwin, *The Voyage of the Beagle*, (E.Z. Publications, 2009)

Heron, *'Love and Possession of the Land'*, *A Beautiful Resistance: The Fire is Here*, (Gods & Radicals, 2016)

Heron (transl), *'Gwyn ap Nudd and Gwyddno Garanhir'*, *The Way of the Awenydd* (website) (2015)

John Rhŷs, *Celtic Folklore, Welsh and Manx*, (Forgotten Books, 2012)

Kim Moore, *If We Could Speak Like Wolves*, (Smith/Doorstop, 2012)

Rachel Bromwich, *'Boddi Maes Gwyddno'*, *The Early Cultures of North-West Europe* (Cambridge, 1950).

Walter Benjamin, *'On the Concept of History'* (website)

William Ashton, *The Evolution of a Coast-Line*, (Forgotten Books, 2015)

Pearl

Rachel Bromwich, '*Boddi Maes Gwyddno*', *The Early Cultures of North-West Europe* (Cambridge, 1950).

Gwyddno's Hamper

Rachel Bromwich (ed.), *The Triads of the Island of Britain*, (University of Wales Press, 2014)

The Crossing of Gwyddno Garanhir

Heron (transl), '*Gwyn ap Nudd and Gwyddno Garanhir*', *The Way of the Awenydd* (website) (2015)

Sea Raven

Charlotte Guest (transl.), '*The Story of Taliesin*', *The Mabinogion*, (Digireads, 2010)

Under a Green Sea

George Walter (ed.), *The Penguin Book of First World War Poetry*, (Penguin, 2006)

Ulf Schmidt, *Secret Science: A Century of Poison Warfare and Human Experiments*, (Oxford University Press, 2015)

Operation Cauldron

Anon, *Operation Cauldron*, (declassified film), (1952)

Tony Wilkins, '*The Would-be Plague Ship - Operation Cauldron and the Carella Incident*', *The Defence of the Realm* (website), (2015)

Stairway to the Stars

Bruce Joel Rubin, *Jacob's Ladder* (film), (1990)

Rob Evans, '*M16 pays out over secret LSD mind control tests*', *The Guardian*, (2006)

Ulf Schmidt, *Secret Science: A Century of Poison Warfare and Human Experiments*, (Oxford University Press, 2015)

Silent Springfields

Anon, '*Stop Moorside: Biggest Nuclear Development in Europe*', *38 Degrees (website)*, (2016)

Marianne Wildart, '*The River Ribble Birthing the Nuclear Nightmare*', *Radiation Free Lakeland* (website), (2014)

Molly Berkemeier, '*Governing Uranium in the United Kingdom*' (DIIS Report, 2014)

Westinghouse Springfields (website)

Toshiba, *Westinghouse Springfields Environmental Report*, (2015)

Cherenkov Blue

Anon, '*First radioactive waste removed from Magnox storage pond*', *World Nuclear News* (website), (2015)

Oliver Tickell, '*Leaked Sellafield Photos Reveal Massive Radioactive Release Threat, The Ecologist* (website), (2014)

Uranium

Albert I. Berger, *Life and Times of the Atomic Bomb*, (Routledge, 2016)

Charlotte Guest (transl.), '*The Story of Taliesin*', *The Mabinogion*, (Digireads, 2010)

Evelyn Mervine, '*Nature's Nuclear Reactors: The Two-Billion-Year-Old Natural Fission Reactors in Gabon, Western Africa*', *Scientific American* (website), (2010)

Marged Haycock, '*Kad Godeu*', '*Preiddu Annwn,*' *Legendary Poems from the Book of Taliesin*, (CMCS, 2007)

Tom Zoellner, *Uranium: War, Energy, and the Rock that Shaped the World*, (Penguin 2009)

Warning Sign

Dr. Derek Muller, *Uranium: Tickling the Dragon's Tail* (film), (World End Entertainment, 2016)

After the Meltdown

John Wendle, '*Animals Rule Chernobyl 30 years after nuclear disaster*', *National Geographic* (website), (2016)

Acknowledgements

Beginning close to home, I'd like to thank my mum and dad for a roof over my head and continuous support; Peter Dillon for discussing ideas, advising, proof-reading and supporting me through the turmoil of the writing process; and the Oak and Feather Grove for steady friendship and inspiration at our seasonal celebrations.

I am indebted to Charlotte Hussey for original work re-imagining the Celtic myths in a modern context. And to Greg Hill for his new translation of 'The Conversation of Gwyn ap Nudd and Gwyddno Garanhir' and recovery of the story of Mererid.

My thanks to Greg, Lee Davies, Rhyd Wildermuth and everyone at Awen ac Awenydd, Dun Brython and Gods & Radicals for publishing and supporting my work, and Korova Poets and Preston Poets' Society for supportive spaces to share my poetry.

My gratitude to fellow Preston-based poet, Nicolas Guy Williams, for teaching me the name of Old Mother Universe and to Kristoffer Hughes for revealing the link between the cauldron and Ceridwen's womb.

I'd also like to thank Tom Brown for his stunning cover art and Nigel at Biddles Books for help assembling the cover and printing the book so quickly and professionally.

A huge thank you to Rhyd Wildermuth and Gods & Radicals Press for publishing my books, first in digital form, and now in print, and for helping me to reach a wider audience.

Finally, my thank you to the Bards and Awenyddion who have kept these stories alive and will carry them into the future.

Lorna Smithers

Lorna is a poet, author, awenydd, Brythonic polytheist, and devotee of Gwyn ap Nudd. Her three books: Enchanting the Shadowlands, The Broken Cauldron, and Gatherer of Souls are published by the Ritona imprint of Gods & Radicals Press. Based in Penwortham, Lancashire, North West England, she is a conservation intern and allotmenteer who is learning to grow small green things and listen to the land. She blogs at 'From Peneverdant.'

RITONA

www.ingramcontent.com/pod-product-compliance
Lightning Source LLC
Chambersburg PA
CBHW072205100526
44589CB00015B/2374
* 9 7 8 1 7 3 5 7 9 4 4 4 0 *